TIME FOR TELLING

•

When an old person dies,
it is as if a whole library
has gone up in flames.
African proverb

For Tom and David M.M.
For my mother, Patricia Williams S.W.

Kingfisher Books, Grisewood & Dempsey Ltd,
Elsley House, 24–30 Great Titchfield Street,
London W1P 7AD

First published in 1991 by Kingfisher Books
Reprinted 1992
This selection copyright © Grisewood & Dempsey Ltd 1991
Illustrations copyright © Sue Williams 1991

The King With Dirty Feet © Pomme Clayton 1991
Loawnu Mends the Sky © Vivienne Corringham 1991
The Old Man Who Wished He Coulda Cry © John Agard 1991
How Turtle Lost Her Sandals © Grace Nichols 1991
The Great Rain © Linda Cotterill 1991
The Big-Wide-Mouthed Toad-Frog © Patrick Ryan 1991
Clever Rabbit and King Lion © Amoafi Kwapong 1991
Half-Chick © Marcus Crouch 1991
The Very Mean King © Sandra A. Agard 1991
Mashenka and the Bear © James Riordan 1991
The Hedley Kow © Maggie Pearson 1991
The Hedgehog's Race © Duncan Williamson 1991
Rainbow Bird © Eric Maddern 1991
Papa Bwa Greedy Guest © Jane Grell 1991
Cherry Tree Hill © Helen East 1991

BRITISH LIBRARY CATALOGUING IN PUBLICATION DATA
Time for telling: a collection of stories from
around the world
I. Medlicott, Mary II. Williams, Sue
808.831

ISBN: 0 86272 804 5

Designed by Caroline Johnson
Edited by Jackie Dobbyne and Karen Gray
Phototypeset by Wyvern Typesetting Ltd
Colour separations by Scantrans Pte Ltd, Singapore
Printed in Spain

Time for Telling

A collection of stories
from around the world

SELECTED BY MARY MEDLICOTT
ILLUSTRATED BY SUE WILLIAMS

Kingfisher Books

Introduction

Time for Telling is a very special book because the stories in it have been written down by real, live storytellers. Real, live storytellers *tell* stories rather than read them aloud. Their stories may be traditional tales, stories they have made up themselves, or stories about things that have happened to them. They may use music, puppets or dance to help tell the story. But the important difference is that, because they do not follow a script, they can be spontaneous; aware of their listeners and of the occasion.

Storytelling is one of the oldest crafts known to human beings. Today's storytellers come from many different backgrounds and cultures and work in many different ways. Some visit schools and libraries, some perform at arts centres. Some work with children, some with adults too. Some tell stories for a living, some for love.

But you don't need to be an 'expert' to tell stories. You don't need to be brilliant at voices or be an actor or actress. What you *do* need is a story to tell and a real wish to tell it so that someone else can know and like it too.

Here is a book full of excellent stories from many different parts of the world where the oral tradition has flourished. Some of these stories are very old. But the people who have written them down for this book know how to make them sound fresh and how to hold children's attention.

You may of course prefer to stick to reading the stories aloud. But if you do want to try to tell one, please feel free to make it your own. You might find yourself cutting one bit, embellishing another. You will certainly want to use your own words. After all, this is what storytellers do and have done throughout history. The story comes out new every time.

And if you do find the time and confidence to tell one of these stories, I'm sure you will be encouraged by your listeners' reactions to tell it again and again.

Mary Medlicott

Contents

The King With Dirty Feet

An Indian tale

●

Pomme Clayton

Once upon a time there was a king. He lived in a hot, dusty village in India. He had everything he wanted and was very happy. But there was one thing that this king hated and that was bathtime.

Perhaps he was a little bit like you?

This king had not washed for a week, he had not washed for a month, he had not washed for a whole year. He had begun to smell. He smelt underneath his arms, in between his toes, behind his ears and up his nose. He was the smelliest king there has ever been. His servants were all very polite about it, but nobody liked to be in the same room as him. Until one day the smell became too much for even the king himself, and he said rather sadly, "I think it is time I had a bath."

He walked slowly down to the river. The villagers whispered, "The king's going to have a bath!" and they rushed down to the river bank to get the best view.

Everyone fell silent when the king stepped into the cool, clear river water. When he called for the royal soap, a huge cheer arose. He washed himself from top to bottom, scrubbed his hair and brushed his teeth. He played with his toy ducks and his little boat.

Then, at last, when he was quite clean, he called for the royal towel and stepped out of the river.

When he had finished drying himself he saw that his feet were covered with dust.

"Oh bother," he cried. "I forgot to wash them." So he stepped back into the water and soaped them well. But as soon as he stood on dry land his feet were dirty again.

"Oh my goodness," he said crossly. "I didn't wash them well enough. Bring me a scrubbing brush." The king scrubbed his feet until they shone. But still, when he stepped on the ground they were dirty.

This time the king was furious. He shouted for his servant, Gabu. Gabu came running and bowed low before the king.

"Gabu," boomed the king, "the king has had a bath, the king is clean, but the earth is dirty. There is dust everywhere. You must clean the earth so there is no more dust and my feet stay clean."

"Yes, Your Majesty," replied Gabu.

"You have three days in which to rid the land of dust, and if you fail do you know what will happen to you?" asked the king.

"No, Your Majesty."

"ZUT!" cried the king.

"ZUT?" said Gabu. "What is ZUT?"

"ZUT is the sound of your head being chopped off."

Gabu began to cry.

"Don't waste time, Gabu. Rid the land of dust at once."

The king marched back to his palace.

"I must put my thinking cap on," said Gabu, and he put his head in his hands and began to think.

"When something is dirty, you brush it."

He asked all the villagers to help him. They took their brushes and brooms and ONE...TWO...THREE...

They all began to sweep – swish, swish, swish, swish, swish – all day long.

Until the dust rose up and filled the air in a thick, dark cloud. Everyone was coughing and spluttering and bumping into each other. The king choked, "Gabu, where are you? I asked you to rid the land of dust, not fill the air with dust. Gabu, you have two more days and ZUT!"

"Oh dear, oh dear," cried Gabu, and put his head in his hands and thought.

"When something is dirty, you wash it."

He asked all the villagers to help him. They took their buckets to the well and filled them up to the brims with water and ONE...TWO...THREE...

They all began to pour – sloosh, sloosh, sloosh, sloosh, sloosh – all day long.

There was so much water it spread across the land. It began to rise. Soon it was up to their ankles, their knees, their waists and then up to their chests.

"Swim everybody," cried Gabu.

The king climbed to the top of the highest mountain where the water lapped his toes and he sniffed, "Gabu, a...atchoo! Where are you?"

Gabu came swimming.

"Yes, Your Majesty?"

"Gabu, I asked you to rid the land of dust not turn our village into a swimming pool. You have one more day and ZUT!"

"Oh dear, oh dear, I have run out of ideas," cried Gabu. The water trickled away and Gabu put his head in his hands and thought.

"I could put the king in an iron room with no windows or doors, chinks or cracks, then no speck of dust could creep in. But I don't think he would like that. Oh, if only I could cover up all the dust with a carpet." Then Gabu had a marvellous idea.

"Of course, why didn't I think of this before? Everyone has a needle and thread and a little piece of leather. Leather is tough, we will cover the land with leather."

He asked all the villagers to help him. Needles were threaded and knots were tied and ONE...TWO...THREE...

They all began to sew – stitch, stitch, stitch, stitch, stitch – all day long.

Then the huge piece of leather was spread across the land and it fitted perfectly. It stretched from the school to the well, from the temple to the palace, and all the way down to the river.

"We've done it," cried Gabu. "I will go and tell the king."

Gabu knocked on the palace door.

"We are ready, Your Majesty."

The king poked his head carefully around the door not knowing what to expect. Then a little smile twitched at the corners of his mouth. The ground looked clean, very clean indeed. He put one foot on the leather and it was spotless. The king walked across the leather.

"This is splendid, comfortable, clean. Well done, Gabu. Well done."

The king turned to the villagers to thank them.

Suddenly, out of the crowd stepped a little old man with a long white beard and a bent back. Everyone had quite forgotten him. He bowed low before the king and spoke in a very quiet voice.

"Your Majesty, how will anything be able to grow now that the land is covered with leather? The grass will not be able to push its way through. There will be no vegetables or flowers and no new trees. The animals will be hungry and there will be nothing for us to eat."

Now everyone was listening.

"Your Majesty, you know you don't have to cover the land with leather to keep your feet clean. It is really quite simple."

The old man took out of his pocket a large pair of scissors. He bent down and began to cut the leather very carefully all around the king's feet. Then he took two laces from his pocket and tied each piece of leather to the king's feet. Then he pulled back the leather that covered the earth and said, "Try them, Your Majesty."

The king looked down at his feet covered in leather and frowned. He had never seen anything like it. He put one foot forward.

"Mmm, very good!" he exclaimed. He took another step.

"This is splendid, comfortable, clean *and* the grass can grow!"

Then the king walked, then he ran and then he jumped.

"Hooray," he cried. "I can walk here, and here, and here. I can walk anywhere and my feet will always be clean."

What was the king wearing on his feet?

That's right, he was wearing SHOES!

They were the first pair of shoes ever to be made, and people have been wearing them ever since.

SNIP, SNAP, SNOUT, MY STORY IS OUT!

Loawnu Mends the Sky

A Chinese story

●

Vivienne Corringham

A long time ago, the world was new. It had just been made, and do you know, they still hadn't got some things in the world exactly right. And one of the things they hadn't got right was the sky. Let me tell you what happened.

One sunny day in China, some children went out to play. They were running around in their favourite field when suddenly – PLOP! – a flat blue thing with raggedy edges fell just near them. Over there – PLOP! – and here – PLOP! – and then – PLOP! PLOP! PLOP! Things were falling all over their field and in the fields around. What do you think they were? The children looked up. Oh, how terrible! Pieces of sky were falling down, and leaving behind great big holes. You could see right inside the sky. Out of the holes oozed thick black clouds spreading like ink in water, and turning the sky from blue to black.

"What shall we do?" they asked each other.

Well, in those days, if you had a problem you went to see the local wise woman, and in this village her name was Loawnu. So they ran up the hill to her house and they rushed through the door, shouting, "Loawnu, what are we going to do? The sky's falling down!"

"Well now," said Loawnu, "why don't you try to find all the pieces of sky that have fallen and then I can mend it."

What a good idea! Off they went and picked up all the bits that were lying on the ground but they couldn't see any more. Can you think of any places where those pieces might be hiding? Yes, they found some down a well, one stuck in a bamboo tree, and another on the roof of a house.

So these friends gathered all the bits they could find – there were lots of them – and carried them up the hill to Loawnu, and she began to count them. It took a long time. Then she went outside and counted the holes in the sky where the bits had fallen out. At the end she said, "I'm afraid there are still some bits missing. Maybe they sank to the bottom of the sea where we'll never find them. I'll put all the pieces you found back into the sky, but we'll need something else to fill in the gaps."

"Why?" asked the children. "Will the gaps matter?"

"Have you ever had a jigsaw puzzle," began Loawnu,

"with a piece missing? You know how it never works without that piece. It's the same with the sky. We'll have to fill in the holes somehow. Ah, but listen! I've had a wonderful idea. Just look at all these coloured stones on the ground."

The children looked around at them.

"That's what I'll use. I can put some red ones in this part of the sky and then, look, I'll use a ring of those purple ones, and maybe I can have some green dots and an orange stripe over there. Won't the sky look pretty!"

But the children's faces had fallen. They wanted a blue sky. "We don't like all those bright colours. The sky's always been blue all day and black all night," they wailed.

Loawnu looked thoughtful for a minute and then she said, "All right. I promise you this. When you wake up tomorrow morning, the sky will be as blue as it always was. Now leave it to me."

So the children went home, and Loawnu built a tall ladder and mended the sky.

The next morning, as soon as the children awoke, they ran out and looked up at the sky. There it was, blue as blue. They couldn't see any holes. They couldn't see any gaps. One little boy went up to Loawnu.

"You're so clever," he said. "I think you used blue cloth and stitched it over the holes. Did you? Did you?"

Loawnu smiled but she said nothing. How do you think she'd done it? Well, she wouldn't tell them and they didn't really mind, because the sky was blue again.

But do you know what happened that night? The smallest girl in the village couldn't sleep because it was too hot. So she went outside for some air, and when she opened the door she couldn't believe her eyes. She could see what Loawnu had used to fill up the holes in the sky, and if you go out at night you'll see too.

Now, I told you the world was still new, and until then the sky had always been plain blue in the day and plain black at night. But it wasn't plain black that night, oh no. The little girl shouted as loudly as she could and the whole village came running. Their mouths fell open with amazement. What do you think they saw?

      S T A R S !

There they were, silver and shining. Loawnu had put one in each of the holes in the sky.

"Aha! That's why she told us to come in the *morning* and the sky would look the same as ever," said one little boy. "It's true, you can't see stars in the daytime, can you, and she didn't say the sky would look the same at night!"

Nobody had ever seen stars before, and so they stood and watched them twinkling and glittering. Some people stayed there all night, and the more they watched, the more they liked them. Everybody agreed the night seemed friendlier now that there were stars.

So that is how Loawnu mended the sky.

The Old Man Who Wished He Coulda Cry

A Caribbean British story

•

John Agard

Once there was a certain old man who wished he coulda cry.

The truth is he had forgotten how to cry.

He longed to hear the sniffling of his tears inside his pillow like when he was a small boy and couldn't get his own way.

All he heard these days was the sound of his footsteps creaking up the steps and the rats tumbling up the old newspapers and carrier bags that he never bothered to throw away.

For a moment the old man thought a cat would do for the rats. But that would mean buying more milk and even cat food, and he was the kind to peel a tangerine in his coat pocket so nobody would ask him for a piece.

But before the thought of a cat had gone out of his head, one sudden scratching started at his door.

From behind his curtain he could see a mannish-face cat

standing with a look as if to say, "I ain't moving till you open this door."

Well, the old man certainly wasn't thinking of letting the cat in, but he just couldn't shut out that look on the cat face.

So he decided to let the cat in, and in no time that cat was diving among the old newspapers and scaring away the rats. Then the cat looked up at the old man as if to say, "What you going to do now?"

"Come on, here's a drop of milk for you, then out you go," was all the old man said.

But as he was putting the cat outside, his blue eyes made four with the cat eyes, and he could swear he saw a teardrop slipping down the cat face.

When he was alone again, the old man thought this was a good moment to cry. Yet his eyes stayed dry as coconut, and as he sat there wishing for tears, suddenly dust started walking all over his bed.

He tried giving the coverlet a good shake-out. But this wasn't any ordinary dust.

This dust was walking over the wallpaper like fine ants, walking over the mirror, and even a photograph the old man had framed of himself in his soldier uniform when he was in the army.

He had to do something about this dust. But there wasn't a single thing his vacuum cleaner could do about it.

Just then he heard a voice calling at the door, "Leh me in. Leh

me in. Fire chase me."

It was a strange voice and it belonged to the strangest broom the old man had ever seen. It had some bristles hard like corncob, some soft like cat fur.

Hear the broom. "Fire chase me. Leh me in." Hear the old man. "I'll let you in if you promise to work for me."

"I promise."

And in no time that runaway broom was swirling up the wall in a horsetail dance till the whole house was whistle bright! The old man couldn't believe he was seeing right. Mirror, bed, everything clean again!

But this wasn't a dream. And the broom standing there, asking for some milk, was as real as anything.

"Fancy that, a broom asking for milk!" the old man say, and he poured a little on a plate just to see what would happen.

To his surprise the broom started to lap up the milk, and the next thing you know, the broom had changed back into the same cat that the old man had put outside.

"Tricky devil," the old man say. "You nearly did fool me, didn't you? But come on, out you go! Out!"

23

The old man pushed the cat out again, and when he went up to his room, he suddenly noticed something. Everywhere was free of dust except for one thing, and that was the photograph of himself in his soldier uniform. Dust was still walking like fine ants over the glass.

The old man looked at the photograph for a long time and wanted to cry. But no eye-water would come.

Then he found himself putting on his going-out shirt, which was unusual for him, because he hardly ever left the house. But he just had to find that cat.

The old man decided to walk down the road. He could see some young people dancing and drinking at the corner.

Suddenly he realized what day it was. August Monday. The long carnival weekend!

And here he was out on the street, looking for a strange cat, when he should be inside his house, away from all the crowds.

But it was too late. When he tried to turn back he found a mass of people coming towards him. Black, white, brown, jumping up with a mad wave of hands, and the costumes giving back brightness to the summer day. The old man felt he'd never escape from this tangle of colour. The crowd was like a big strong wind sweeping him along.

And from the top of a truck, a band beating drums of steel sent a sweet deafness through the old man head. Even so he heard a voice behind him say:

"Papa Doo-Doo
Papa Doo-Doo
Move yu foot
Till yu feel like new."

The old man recognize that voice. It was the voice of the cat. But when he turn around, all he see was somebody, he couldn't tell if it was a man or a woman, dressed up in cat costume, and waving a long broom to the beat of the music.

"Papa Doo-Doo
Papa Doo-Doo
Move yu foot
Till yu feel like new."

The old man was sure – sure the voice was the same, but by now the cat-dancer had disappeared into the crowd.

Meantime, something was happening to the old man. See he moving to the music, yes, and in all that crowd of dancing black, white, brown, the old man could feel a wet trickle running down he cheek. And when he put up a hand, it wasn't sweat.

The old man couldn't believe he was crying small boy tears again. He couldn't remember the last day he feel so good.

The Great Rain

A Native American Indian legend

 Linda Cotterill

It was very strange weather. Purple and black clouds raced and tumbled across the sky. They hid the sun, they hid the mountain tops. Inside the clouds lightning flashed and thunder rumbled. Nokomis, the Great Earth Spirit, watched the sky and was worried.

"This isn't the right weather for summer," she thought. "Why is the Thunderbird making it so dark and stormy? Thunderbird!" she called. "What's wrong?"

"Kaaa!" screeched a voice inside the clouds. "I'll tell you what's wrong! I'm angry!"

There was a flash of lightning and the clouds tore apart.

Nokomis could see the Thunderbird crouching over the mountains, his talons gripping their tops, his open wings stretching from horizon to horizon.

"Very angry!" he shouted, and lightning darted from his red eyes.

"But why are you angry?" asked Nokomis.

"Why?" He glared down at her, stretching his neck and rattling his wings to send thunder rolling about the sky.

"I'm angry because the people love you and they don't love me!"

"They love me because I'm the earth, their home," Nokomis said. "I'm the rivers where they fish, the forests where they hunt and the plains where they pitch their teepees. They dance and give thanks to you for the rain you send," she reminded him.

"But they love you best!" He beat his wings until the thunder shook the mountainside.

"I'll show them. I'll send them so much rain that the rivers will flood and cover their forests and their plains and their teepees. Everyone will drown. Then they'll be sorry! Kaaa!" He screamed, stretching wide his eagle beak, then pulled the black clouds over himself again.

"Thunderbird, Thunderbird," called Nokomis, but he would not answer.

Nokomis was very worried. "What am I going to do?" she thought. "He won't talk to me. And he won't change his mind. I know him. He'll just sulk up there getting angrier and angrier until he's ready to burst. Then he'll do what he said – make it rain and rain."

She looked at the mountain where Thunderbird was hiding and thought hard.

"I don't think he can make enough rain to cover everything. Not everything. Not the mountains. Yes! That's it!"

Nokomis called. "Listen to me, all you animals and people, there is going to be a terrible flood. You must go high up in the mountains, you'll be safe there. You must go quickly." Her voice travelled everywhere. In the grass jackrabbits heard her and stopped nibbling. Beneath the ground moles heard her and stopped digging. Under the water beavers heard her and stopped building their dam. Soon all the animals and insects were flying, running and hopping to the mountains.

It was only the people who took no notice. In their villages they went on sewing moccasins, making arrows and looking at the sky.

"It's too noisy in those villages – everyone talking – they can't hear me," Nokomis thought. "I must find someone quiet to tell."

In the long grass she saw a boy looking for rabbits. Not a twig snapped, not a blade of grass squeaked as he crept forward, an arrow ready in his bow.

"It's Blue Jay," smiled Nokomis. "He's as silent as a shadow, he'll hear me. Blue Jay! Blue Jay!" she called, but he didn't seem to hear. He went on quietly slipping through the grass. Nokomis called louder, "Blue Jay, you must tell your family and everyone to go into the mountains."

But Blue Jay thought her voice was only the sound of the wind.

"How noisy the wind is today – shaking the trees and rattling the bushes. It will frighten away all the rabbits," he thought and carried on hunting.

"How deaf these humans are!" said Nokomis. "Who else can I tell?"

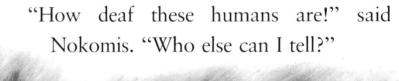

By the river she saw a girl. With her fish-spear ready she crouched barefooted on a rock. She was waiting for a speckled trout to come out of the weeds.

"It's Little Otter," smiled Nokomis. "She's as silent as that rock – she'll hear me."

Just to make sure this time she called very loudly, "Little Otter, Little Otter!"

But Little Otter took no notice. She had seen the shadow of a fish. Holding her breath she leant forward and lifted her spear above her head. She stared hard into the water and didn't look round.

"Little Otter!" Nokomis called again. "You must listen to me – there isn't much time – listen to me – Little Otter – listen to me!" But Little Otter thought her voice was only the sound of the river.

"How noisy the water is today clattering and chattering over the stones. It will frighten away all the fish," she thought and carried on fishing.

Nokomis was puzzled. "These humans only seem to understand their own language. I must find some other way to warn them, something they will understand."

She frowned up at the sky. It was much darker and behind the clouds thunder muttered. Soon the Thunderbird would start the rain.

A little while later an old woman strode into the village where Blue Jay and Little Otter lived. She was tall and thin. Her face and hands were wrinkled like bark. She wore a dress of soft green buckskin with fringes down the sleeves and brown moccasins embroidered with flowers. Her grey hair hung in a long plait and in her headband was one eagle feather dyed red.

32

Gathering all the people round her she said, "The Thunderbird is very angry. He is going to make so much rain that all this land will be covered with water. If you stay here you'll drown, but in the mountains you'll be safe."

No one in the village had seen the old woman before, but her face and eyes were very old and very wise so they believed her. They folded their teepees, stamped out their cooking fires, packed pots and blankets and babies into carrying baskets and went into the mountains.

All that day the old woman hurried from village to village warning people. Soon almost all the people were safe in the mountains. There was only one village left to tell.

As the old woman came near she heard drumming and singing. The people were having a feast. In the centre of the teepees people were dancing, stamping their feet and jumping high into the air. Some had drums and others had rattles made from dried seed pods and shells tied on to sticks. The noise was louder than the thunder.

No one noticed the old woman come into the village. She called to the dancers, "Listen to me, people!" but they danced on. "If those drums stopped they could hear me," she said, but the drummers said, "This is dancing time, Grandma," and drummed louder.

"Maybe just one person will listen," she thought. She tried to grab a man dancing by. He pulled his arm away and yelled at her, "Leave me alone, old woman! Can't you see I'm dancing!"

The old woman was getting angry. She pushed her way through the dancers. She was very strong for such an old woman. She stood in the centre of the dancers and shouted.

"A terrible storm is coming. The water will cover the tops of the tallest trees."

The people only laughed. "That will be very wet indeed, old woman! You had better run away quickly or you will be drowned."

"If you don't go to the mountains it is you who will be drowned," said the old woman. "Look at the sky, see how angry the Thunderbird is."

The sky was full of red and black clouds.

"How does an old woman like you know what the Thunderbird is feeling? Go away!" they shouted. "You are spoiling our dancing."

They made a circle and twisted and turned around her, singing and laughing. When she tried to speak again they shook their rattles at her. They pushed her and bumped her.

They were making so much noise that they didn't hear the Thunderbird leap into the air and fly.

"Kaaa!" he screamed. "Kaaa!"

When thunder boomed and roared from his wings they only shook their rattles and shouted louder than ever.

When the lightning crackled and jumped they leapt higher and shouted, "See! See! The lightning is dancing with us!"

Even when the rain began to fall, faster and faster, in bigger and bigger drops, they only danced wilder than ever. They whirled and pranced, spinning and kicking.

The old woman watched them. Suddenly she raised her arms and shouted. Her voice was louder than the thunder. It was like a great wind tearing up trees and blowing down mountains.

The dancers and drummers froze. They looked at her with wide-open eyes and mouths.

"So you only want to dance and shake your rattles, eh?" she said. "You deserve to drown, all of you! But I am Nokomis your Mother, so I will save you. But I will also change you. From this day you will always carry your rattles and whenever you see a human you will dance and shake them. Just as you did today to an old woman who tried to help you."

As Nokomis spoke, the people began to shrink. They grew smaller and thinner then they began to curl over and crumple. Soon there was no longer a circle of dancers round her but a circle of snakes.

"Now I must take you all to the mountains," she said, piling them into a large basket.

It rained for days and weeks. Just as the Thunderbird had threatened, the forest and the plains were covered with water. But up in the mountains the animals and people were safe.

When the rain stopped the water drained away. Soon everybody went back to their homes.

Including the snakes. They went far away from rain and lived in dry places. And whenever they see a human they raise their heads, sway as if they were dancing and shake their rattles which they carry in their tails.

And that is how Nokomis the Great Earth Spirit brought rattlesnakes into the world.

How Turtle Lost Her Sandals

An Amerindian legend from Guyana

•

Grace Nichols

Once upon a long ago time Turtle was one of the fastest animals in all the land though you wouldn't believe it by looking at her now, moving about like a slow-coach. Well, Turtle was fast in those days because, you see, she had two fine pairs of hoofs which took her wherever she wanted to go in no time, even though her legs were short. Turtle was very proud of her beautiful hoofs which she used to call 'my sandals'.

Now, a lot of animals were jealous of Turtle and her sandals but one animal who was really really jealous of Turtle was Deer. Yes, Deer, my dear children. Deer was very slow in that long ago time because she had claws at the end of her feet instead of hoofs and she moved about in a slow scraping kind of way.

Oh, many a day you could see Deer admiring her antlers in a stream but whenever she looked down at her feet she would get annoyed and think, "If only I had fast hoofs like that stupid low-down Turtle to run like a fire through the forest." The more Deer thought about Turtle's beautiful hoofs the more jealous she became until one day she thought of a plan to get Turtle's hoofs.

It was a hot sunny morning and Turtle was resting under the shade of a big tree when who should come up to her?

"Good morning, Turtle," Deer said in her sweetest voice.

"Oh, good morning, Deer," said Turtle, who was really surprised since Deer had never stopped to talk to her before.

"It's a fine morning," Deer said, brightly.

"Yes," replied Turtle, beginning to wonder what Deer really wanted. Nearly every morning was fine in their part of the world.

After a little pause Deer looked down at Turtle's hoofs as if she was seeing them for the first time.

"What a beautiful pair of sandals you have," she exclaimed.

"Yes, they're lovely, even though I say so myself," agreed Turtle, feeling nice that someone liked her sandals.

Then Deer put on her most pleading voice and said, "Oh, Turtle, please let me have a try of your sandals. It will give me such pleasure to move quickly for a change. You can't imagine what it's like crawling about all the time and I would be back before you could even call my name."

"Please, Turtle," Deer begged again, "just for a minute."

Turtle didn't like parting with her precious sandals but she felt sorry for Deer and after a while she bent down to unclip them.

"Please bring them back fast," she said, handing over her sandal-hoofs.

Deer put them on quickly. She ran like the fire. She ran like the wind. Deer was so delighted with the sandals that she decided she was never going to give them back to Turtle.

Meanwhile, Turtle waited on Deer to return her beautiful sandals. She waited and she waited and she waited. After many days of waiting, Turtle knew that Deer wasn't going to return her sandals. At long last Turtle did the only thing she could do. Slowly she fitted on the claws that Deer had left behind.

But it is said that from that day to today Turtle is still hoping that Deer will bring back her sandals. And while Deer runs like the fire and the wind through the forest poor Turtle crawls about ever so slow. Poking her head out at times, listening and waiting, listening and waiting.

The Big-Wide-Mouthed Toad-Frog

A North American story

•

Patrick Ryan

One fine day long ago when birds did talk and beasts did sing and grasshoppers did spit tobacco, two young ones named Jack and Mary went out for a walk.

Jack and Mary walked for the longest time. They walked further than you could tell me and further than I could tell you. They walked up over hills and mountains and down through the dark green woods. And as they walked, they talked.

"Ah now, Jack," says Mary. "Wouldn't it be good if we should catch a creature and keep it as a pet?"

"Ah now, Mary," says Jack. "It would be good. But what creature shall we catch?"

"One not very big," declared Mary.

"Nor very small," declared Jack.

"One not very tame," cried Mary.

"Yet not very wild," cried Jack.

"Well, there's only one thing to do," said Mary.

"And what is that?" asked Jack.

"Set a trip-trap," Mary said, "to catch a creature to be our pet. And I know how to do just that."

So Mary showed Jack how to set a trip-trap. Twelve sticks they gathered from the green-willow tree, long and strong and narrow as could be. Mary gathered six sticks and Jack a half-a-dozen more, and they wove together the first four. The next four sticks round the first ones were bound, and the last four tied the trigger for the trip-trap down.

Then Jack went home, and so did Mary. They left the trip-trap sit for all the night. Come the morning light the two friends ran, over hill and mountain, into the dark green wood, to see what creature the trip-trap did trap.

And lo and behold the creature it held was not very big nor yet very small, neither tame nor wild was it. It was round and wet and slimy and green, with tiny eyes and great big hind legs, and the widest big-wide mouth that ever was seen.

"Look!" said Mary.

"Look!" said Jack.

"Our trip-trap has trapped a round, wet, slimy, green BIG-WIDE-MOUTHED TOAD-FROG!'

And so it had.

And Jack and Mary they lifted the trap, and the BIG-WIDE-MOUTHED TOAD-FROG jumped and skipped and hopped right out of that.

"HELLO! (gulp) HELLO! (gulp) HELLO!" shouted the Big-Wide-Mouthed Toad-Frog. "WHAT ARE YOU AND WHAT DO YOU EAT?"

"How-do," said Mary. "I'm a little girl named Mary. And I like to eat nuts and berries and apples and cherries and hominy and corn pone and succotash and sandwiches of cheese and fish and chips and ice cream and cake."

"(Gulp) OOOOO...! (gulp) AAAAAHH! (gulp) A-MAZ-ING!" said the Big-Wide-Mouthed Toad-Frog.

"Well-now," said Jack. "I'm a little boy named Jack. And I do like to eat grits and johnny cake and cracker jack and apple-y pie and peach-y cobbler and buttermilk biscuits and sausages and rashers and chips and peas and spinach and lettuce and carrots and candy-sweets."

"(Gulp) OOOOO...! (gulp) AAAAAHH! (gulp) A-MAZ-ING!" said the Big-Wide-Mouthed Toad-Frog. "WELL, (gulp) I MUST BE OFF (gulp) AND AWAY! (gulp)"

And before Jack and Mary could catch the Big-Wide-Mouthed Toad-Frog for to keep him as a pet, he was up and away with a hop, a skip, and a jump, for the Big-Wide-Mouthed Toad-Frog he wanted to see the Big-Wide-World.

44

Now the very first strange creature that the Big-Wide-Mouthed Toad-Frog did meet in his travels round the Big-Wide-World was a Big-Old-Brown-Fat Monster with Branches growing out of the side of her head.

"(Gulp) HELLO! (gulp) HELLO! (gulp) HELLO!" shouted the Big-Wide-Mouthed Toad-Frog. "WHAT ARE YOU AND WHAT DO YOU EAT?"

And the Monster she Moo-ed and she Moo-ed and she Moo-ed. "I am a Cow," she said. "And I like to eat thistles the colour of bright blue, and grasses and four-leaf clovers, too."

"(Gulp) OOOOO...! (gulp) AAAAAHH! (gulp) A-MAZ-ING!" shouted the Big-Wide-Mouthed Toad-Frog.

And he hopped and skipped and jumped his way on through the Big-Wide-World.

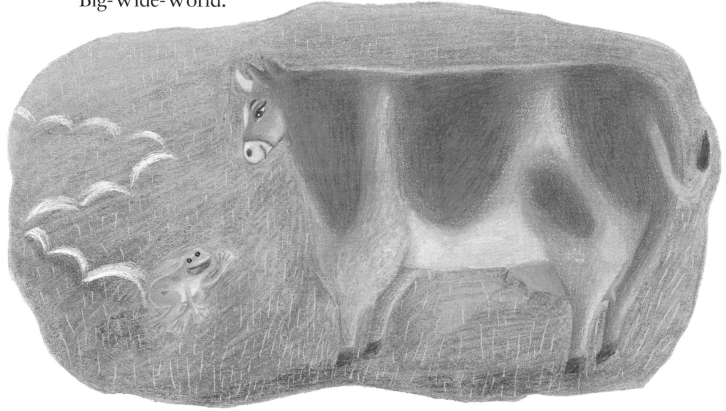

And the very next wondrous strange creature that the Big-Wide-Mouthed Toad-Frog did meet in his travels round the Big-Wide-World was a Funny Little Thing that hung upside down and had Two Heads.

"(Gulp) HELLO! (gulp) HELLO! (gulp) HELLO!" shouted the Big-Wide-Mouthed Toad-Frog. "WHAT ARE YOU AND WHAT DO YOU EAT?"

"Ho-hum," yawned the creature. Hum-ho. I'm an opossum."

"Ho-hum," yawned the baby Opossum in his mama's pouch. "Hum-ho. Me too."

"We like to eat berries and cherries and roots and twigs," they replied.

"(Gulp) OOOOO...! (gulp) AAAAAHH! (gulp) A-MAZ-ING!" shouted the Big-Wide-Mouthed Toad-Frog.

And he hopped and skipped and jumped his way on through the Big-Wide-World.

So the next Odd Beast that he saw was as Big as a Mountain and covered with a Fur Rug.

"(Gulp) HELLO! (gulp) HELLO! (gulp) HELLO!" shouted the Big-Wide-Mouthed Toad-Frog. "WHAT ARE YOU AND WHAT DO YOU EAT?"

46

"Grrrr!" growled the beast. "I'm a Big Brown Bear. And I love to eat honey and fish and more fish and more honey."

"(Gulp) OOOOO...! (gulp) AAAAAHH! (gulp) A-MAZ-ING!" shouted the Big-Wide-Mouthed Toad-Frog.

And he hopped and skipped and jumped his way on through the Big-Wide-World.

Well, the next Queer Creature the Big-Wide-Mouthed Toad-Frog did meet in his journey across the Big-Wide-World was a Scary-Looking-Fellow with a Bushy-Stripy Tail and a Black Mask round his eyes – just like a robber bandit!

"(Gulp) HELLO! (gulp) HELLO! (gulp) HELLO!" shouted the Big-Wide-Mouthed Toad-Frog. "WHAT ARE YOU AND WHAT DO YOU EAT?"

And the fellow told him, "I'm a raccoon. I love to eat GARBAGE, RUBBISH and TRASH, the smellier the better!"

"(Gulp) OOOOO...! (gulp) AAAAAHH! (gulp) DIS-GUS-TING!" shouted the Big-Wide-Mouthed Toad-Frog.

And he hopped and skipped and jumped his way on through the Big-Wide-World.

Now the last monstrous beast the Big-Wide-Mouthed Toad-Frog did spy on his travels was a Long Green Log with a Great Big Smile who rolled and slithered along on his belly.

"(Gulp) HELLO! (gulp) HELLO! (gulp) HELLO!" shouted the Big-Wide-Mouthed Toad-Frog. "WHAT ARE YOU AND WHAT DO YOU EAT?"

And the Smiling Log smiled a Great-Big-Wide-Mouthed Smile and he said, "Heh heh heh. I'm an alligator! And I just LOVE to eat BIG-WIDE-MOUTHED TOAD-FROGS!" said the alligator. "Have YOU seen any BIG-WIDE-MOUTHED TOAD-FROGS about?"

And the Big-Wide-Mouthed Toad-Frog's eyes got VERY VERY BIG and his Big-Wide-Mouth closed up and got very very small and the Big-Wide-Mouthed Toad-Frog said with a squeak, "Nope, I've not seen any such thing as a Big-Wide-Mouthed Toad-Frog ever, not at all round here, not ever in all my life!'

Then the Big-Wide-Mouthed Toad-Frog hopped and skipped and jumped his way all the way back to Jack and Mary's trip-trap, as fast as he could hop and skip and jump. And in that trip-trap he stayed most merrily, and lived there a most long time for his life, because the Big-Wide-Mouthed Toad-Frog had learned an ever so important lesson: that it sometimes pays to keep a BIG WIDE MOUTH SHUT!

The Very Mean King

A Kenyan story

•

Sandra A. Agard

There was once a Very Mean King
who sat on his throne all day long
and laughed in a wicked way.
HEE, HEE, HEE.
When he was not laughing,
he was rubbing his hands together.
RUB, RUB, RUB.
When he was not rubbing his hands
together, he was stamping his feet.
STAMP, STAMP, STAMP.
And when he was not stamping his feet, he was growling.
GROWL, GROWL, GROWL.

He never smiled.

He never laughed.

He never danced.

And because he never smiled, laughed or danced, he never allowed his people to smile, laugh or dance.

In fact, he had some very mean-looking guards who snarled and hissed all day. SNARL, SNARL, HISS, HISS. And if the Very Mean King caught anyone smiling, laughing or dancing he would order his very mean-looking guards to whip the people.
WHIP, WHIP, WHIP.

So the people were sad all the time and were made to work in the Very Mean King's fields all day long under the burning hot sun.

Sometimes the Very Mean King would not let the people stop to rest or give them anything to eat. And when the people begged for food – what do you think? The Very Mean King said "NO!" in a very loud voice.

What a Very Mean King!

One day the Very Mean King slept after an enormous lunch.
SNORE, SNORE, SNORE.

And the guards guarded, looking as mean as ever.

Up in the sky there lived the Sparrow who had been watching the earth for a long time and had seen how meanly the Very Mean King was treating his people. So she decided it was time the Very Mean King was taught a lesson.

So from its very special secret place amongst the clouds she took the Rattle of Punishment and flew down to earth.

She cast a very special secret spell that made her invisible and as she flew the Rattle began to play beautiful music. When the people heard the music they instantly stopped what they were

doing and found that their lips began to twitch, their feet were tingling and their hips began to wriggle and before they could stop themselves they were smiling, laughing and dancing.

They could not stop.

They smiled and smiled.

They laughed and laughed.

They danced and danced all over the Very Mean King's fields.

Well, the smiling, laughing and dancing woke up the Very Mean King and when he looked out of the window and saw what the people were doing he sent his mean-looking guards out to stop them.

But no sooner had the guards arrived at the fields, they too began to smile, laugh and dance.

So the Very Mean King went himself and in a loud voice shouted, "STOP!"

He shouted so loud it shook the very foundations of the earth.

The Sparrow stopped playing and everybody stopped smiling, laughing and dancing. They ran away and hid.

The Very Mean King looked at his fields. They were all trampled and completely ruined.

This time he roared a huge roar, "ROARRRRRR!"

And he was just about to call out his army to capture the people when the Sparrow appeared before him and said, "You have been a very mean king and for that you will be punished."

And she shook the Rattle of Punishment and this time only the Very Mean King smiled, laughed or danced.

He smiled, laughed and danced for THREE DAYS and THREE NIGHTS until he begged the Sparrow to stop.

He fell on the ground exhausted.

The people came out of their hiding places and waited.

The Very Mean King got up and looked at his people. He remembered how happy they had seemed when they smiled, laughed and danced and he bowed his head in shame. Then, in a very kingly voice, he said, "My people, I've been a very mean king. From now on I'm going to be a good king."

So he gave his people food and they smiled, laughed and danced. So did the guards, for they were getting a little tired of snarling and hissing all day and had rather enjoyed singing, laughing and dancing in the fields.

The Sparrow flew away taking with her the magic Rattle of Punishment, placing it back in its special secret place.

But who knows when she might come back again and who will dance that special magic dance?

COULD IT BE YOU?

Clever Rabbit and King Lion

A story from Ghana

•

Amoafi Kwapong

Once upon a time, and a very good time it was, there lived in the rainforest of Ghana many animals and Lion was their king.

King Lion lived in the best cave on one side of the forest while the rest of the animals shared the other side. The other animals were not amused but they had no choice than to remain where they were.

Clever Rabbit was a very close friend of Madam Hare. Clever Rabbit was very quick at solving problems and riddles which earned her the title of 'Clever'. Madam Hare was known in the whole wide forest as a kind-hearted lady. With her long ears, Madam Hare could hear a long way away.

One day, Madam Hare overheard King Lion talking to his wife. He was boasting about a plan of his to eat up Clever Rabbit. He had already eaten most of the little animals in the forest.

"Today," he said, "it's Clever Rabbit's turn."

Madam Hare was very upset. She hurried to tell Clever Rabbit what she had heard. At first Clever Rabbit was very upset too. She thought to herself, "I mind my own business and I don't deserve this." Madam Hare tried to console her, but Clever Rabbit said, "Action is what I need."

Clever Rabbit had a quick think and she came up with an idea.

"I'll go to King Lion's cave and offer myself to him. I bet he'll be so angry and confused he won't eat me just yet."

"Very good," replied Madam Hare.

Clever Rabbit set out for King Lion's cave.

Meanwhile, King Lion was on his way to Clever Rabbit's burrow. Halfway down the path, King Lion and Clever Rabbit met face to face. King Lion's eyes were red and he looked fierce. Clever Rabbit put on a brave face and a smile. She greeted King Lion, "Good morning, Your Majesty. I heard you were going to eat me up for dinner today. So I wanted to make it easier for you by offering myself to you."

"Don't be cheeky, you little rascal," answered King Lion.

Clever Rabbit continued, "I didn't mean to be cheeky, Your Majesty, but on second thoughts I don't think you'll enjoy eating me just yet. Give me three weeks to fatten up for you. You see, I'm all bones."

"Very well," retorted King Lion. "I can wait three weeks."

So off went Clever Rabbit to her burrow, stopping on the way to tell Madam Hare the good news. "Hooray! Hooray!" cried the two friends.

A week passed but Clever Rabbit looked the same. A second week passed and still Clever Rabbit had not added an ounce of flesh to her skinny body.

After two weeks King Lion began to count the seconds, the minutes, the hours. Day one came and went. Then it was day two, day three, day four, day five, day six and day seven!

"Three weeks are up! I'm going to feast on rabbit today!" gloated King Lion.

Clever Rabbit dressed in her prettiest clothes with bows in her hair. On her way to King Lion's cave she stopped to chat with Madam Hare. Madam Hare wished Clever Rabbit the best of luck saying, "I trust that you'll come back again."

"Thank you," said Clever Rabbit, "I certainly need a lot of luck today." And off she went.

When she arrived at King Lion's cave, King Lion was working up his appetite. He was just about to pounce on Clever Rabbit when she said, "Oh, Your Majesty, you should hear this! There's a *bigger* lion not too far away from here who's been competing with you. He's eating all the little animals there and I hear he's eaten more than you have."

"Is that so?" said King Lion. "Show me the way to this arrogant lion and I'll soon sort him out."

Clever Rabbit led the way. She was so overjoyed at not being gobbled up by King Lion that she began to sing, dance and skip along the path. King Lion was not amused. He roared at Clever Rabbit, "Stop singing, dancing and skipping at once!" Clever Rabbit stopped at once.

Soon they were both standing by a lake. Clever Rabbit pointed to a spot where King Lion should stand and look in the water. King Lion quickly stood on that spot and stretched to look in the water. There was another lion! Quick as a flash, King Lion jumped into the lake to fight the other lion.

Too late, he realized that Clever Rabbit had tricked him! He struggled to get out of the water. But as you and I know, cats (even big cats) can't swim too well. King Lion drowned and Clever Rabbit was free to sing, dance and skip again. She sang and danced and skipped all the way back to Madam Hare who was waiting anxiously.

Clever Rabbit and Madam Hare sang, danced and skipped together all night long. And when the other little animals of the rainforest heard what had happened, they hurried to join in the celebration.

The story that you've just heard, take it with you and share it.

Half-Chick

A tale from Spain

•

Marcus Crouch

Once there was a hen who was no different from any other of her kind, and she had hatched out many broods of pretty chicks. What went wrong, I don't know, but when one of her eggs cracked open out came a half-chick. He had only one leg and one wing and one eye.

His mother was a good hen. She might have felt like pushing the ugly thing out of the nest, but instead she gave him more than half the love she gave the rest of her family.

But Half-Chick was hard to love. It was not just that he looked so odd. He was full of mischief. Every day he played tricks on his mother and his brothers and sisters until the poor hen was in despair.

A day came when Half-Chick hopped up to her on his one leg

and said, "I'm tired of home. Nothing ever happens. I am going out to see the world."

"Where will you go, my chick?"

"I am off to Madrid to see the King. Goodbye, Mother."

And Half-Chick hopped out of the farmyard and into the wide world.

He came to a little stream. It should have been singing as it raced to the sea but thick weeds had choked it.

"Ah, Half-Chick," said the stream. "You are just what I need. Peck away these weeds and let me out of my prison."

"Sorry," said Half-Chick, " I can't stop. I'm on my way to see the King." And he left the stream as helpless as ever.

His way lay through a wood, and he came to a place where foresters had lit a fire. Now the fire was almost out. It was dying for want of twigs to keep it alight.

"Dear Half-Chick," said the fire.

"Save me. Just pick up a few sticks in
your beak and drop them into my heart."

"I'd like to help," said Half-Chick, "but it is getting
late and I must get to Madrid. Someone else will be along
very soon."

He hopped on, making very good progress on only one
leg. In the distance he saw the spires and towers of Madrid. The
sight spurred him on, and he hopped even faster.

There was a big tree by the roadside, swaying and tossing
violently. Out of the tree came the voice of the wind, which had
got itself entangled in the branches.

"Help!" called the wind. "Fly up into the tree and let me
out, and I will be your friend for ever."

"No time," said Half-Chick. "I mustn't keep
the King waiting."

On through the city streets he hopped. Some people stared in amazement, but most of them took no notice. They were used to strange sights in the city. The palace walls were close now. Guards stood at the gates. They let him past without a word, and he supposed that they had their orders to let him in. By chance, he had come in through the servants' entrance. The kitchen was nearby, and the first person he saw was the cook in his white apron and tall hat.

"This must be the King," thought Half-Chick. "What a strange crown he is wearing."

He saluted the cook respectfully with his wing. The cook looked down at the funny little creature. "Well, well," he said. "You won't make even half a meal, but I mustn't grumble." And he grabbed Half-Chick and dropped him into a pot that was boiling on the fire.

"Water, water!" screamed Half-Chick. "You are hurting me. Let me out."

"You didn't help me when I was choking with weeds. Why should I help you?" said the water. And it bubbled faster than before.

"Fire, fire, spare me!" said Half-Chick.

"Did you spare me when all I needed was a couple of sticks?" said the fire. And it blazed more fiercely than ever.

A howling wind came from the chimney. Half-Chick called, "Wind, wind! Blow the fire out and cool the water. You are the only friend I have left."

"So I am your friend, am I?" said the wind. "Very well, old friends should help one another." And it blew down the chimney, scooped Half-Chick out of the cooking pot, and swept him up into the air.

Over the roofs of Madrid sailed the wind and Half-Chick, up and up until the King's palace seemed no bigger than a cottage.

"Do you remember, my friend," said the wind, "who was caught in a tree? And who was too busy to help?"

Then the wind swooped down and landed on top of the tallest spire of the cathedral.

"This is where you belong," said the wind, and away it blew leaving Half-Chick stuck on the spire.

Half-Chick is still there. As the winds blow he turns and points out the direction to the people below. Sometimes a sound drifts down to them and they say, "That weathercock must be getting rusty. Listen to him creaking."

But really it is Half-Chick weeping and saying to the world, "How sorry I am! Why wasn't I a better bird?"

Why indeed!

Mashenka and the Bear

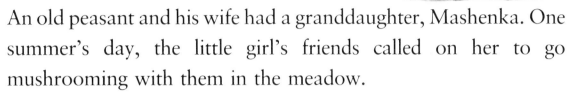

A Russian story

•

James Riordan

An old peasant and his wife had a granddaughter, Mashenka. One summer's day, the little girl's friends called on her to go mushrooming with them in the meadow.

"Grannie, Grandad," cried Mashenka. "May I go out to play? I'll bring you lots of mushrooms, I promise."

"Run along then," the old pair said, "but mind you don't go near the forest or else the wolves or bears will get you."

Off skipped the girls towards the meadow at the forest edge. Mashenka knew that the best and biggest mushrooms grew beneath the trees and bushes in the forest. Almost without noticing it, she wandered out of sight of her friends. She moved from tree to tree, from bush to bush, picking a basketful of mushrooms – reds and yellows, browns and whites. All the while she went deeper and deeper into the forest. Suddenly, she looked up and realized she was lost.

"Hell-oooo! Hell-oooo!" she called.

There was no reply.

Someone heard her nonetheless.

From the trees came a rustling and a cracking, and out stepped a big brown bear. When he set eyes on the little girl, he threw up his arms in joy.

"Aha!" he cried. "You'll make a fine servant for me, my pretty one."

Taking the girl roughly by the arm, he dragged her to his cottage in the depths of the dark wood. Once inside, he growled at her, "Now stoke the fire, cook some porridge and make my home clean and tidy."

There now began a miserable life in the bear's cottage for poor Mashenka. Day after day she toiled from dawn to dusk, afraid the bear would eat her. All the while she thought of how she could escape. Finally, an idea came to her.

"Mister Bear," she said politely, "may I go home for a day to show my grandparents I am alive and well?"

"Certainly not," growled the bear. "You'll never leave here. If you have a message I'll take it myself."

That was just what Mashenka had planned. She baked some cherry pies, piled them on a dish and fetched a big basket. Then she called the bear.

"Mister Bear, I'll put the pies in this basket for you to carry home. Remember, though, not to open the basket and don't touch the pies. I'll be watching. When you set off I'll climb on to the roof to keep an eye on you."

"All right, pretty one," grumbled the bear. "Just let me take a nap before I go."

No sooner was the bear asleep than Mashenka quickly climbed on to the roof and made a lifelike figure out of a pole, her coat and headscarf. Then she scrambled down, squeezed into the basket and pulled the dish of cherry pies over her head. When the bear woke up and saw the basket ready, he hoisted it on to his broad back and set off for the village.

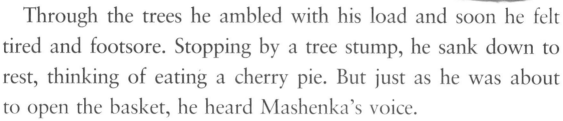

Through the trees he ambled with his load and soon he felt tired and footsore. Stopping by a tree stump, he sank down to rest, thinking of eating a cherry pie. But just as he was about to open the basket, he heard Mashenka's voice.

"Don't sit there all day and don't you touch those pies."

Glancing round he could just see her figure on his roof.

"My, my, that maid has sharp eyes," he mumbled to himself.

Up he got and continued on his way.

On and on he went, carrying the heavy load. Soon he came upon another tree stump.

"I'll just take a rest and eat a cherry pie," he thought, puffing and panting. Yet once again Mashenka's muffled voice was heard.

"Don't sit down and don't touch those pies. Go straight to the village as I told you."

He looked back but could no longer see his house.

"Well, I'll be jiggered!" he exclaimed. "She's got eyes like a hawk, that girl."

So on he went.

Through the trees he shuffled, down into the valley, on through groves of ash, up grassy knolls until, finally, he emerged into a meadow.

"I must rest my poor feet," he sighed. "And I'll just have one small pie to refresh me. She surely cannot see me now."

But from out of nowhere came a distant voice.

"I can see you! I can see you! Don't you touch those cherry pies! Go on, Mister Bear."

The bear was puzzled, even scared.

"What an extraordinary girl she is," he growled, hurrying across the field.

At last he arrived at the village, stopped at Mashenka's door and knocked loudly.

"Open up, open up!" he cried gruffly. "I've brought a present from your granddaughter."

The moment they heard his voice, however, dogs came running from all the yards. Their barking startled him so much, he left the basket at the door and made off towards the forest without a backward glance.

How surprised Mashenka's grandparents were when they opened the door, found the basket and saw no one in sight.

Grandad lifted up the lid, stared hard and could scarcely believe his eyes. For there beneath the cherry pies sat the little girl, alive and well.

Grannie and Grandad both danced with joy, hugged Mashenka and said what a clever girl she was to trick the bear. Soon all her friends heard the news and came running to hug and kiss her too. Mashenka was so happy.

In the meantime, deep in the forest, the old bear had reached home and shouted to the figure on the roof to make his tea. Of course, it did not take him long to learn that the wise young girl had tricked him.

The Hedley Kow

An English story

●

Maggie Pearson

What sort of creature is the Hedley Kow? It's not a cow, that's for sure – well, only sometimes. Sometimes it looks like a cow.

Sometimes like a horse – and a very fine horse, too, until you try to ride it. Then it's likely to turn itself into a bale of straw, or a pool of water, or... You may see the Hedley Kow and never know it: who's to say?

There was an old woman who made ends meet as best she could. A bit of sewing here. A bit of apple-picking there. A bit of mowing in some other place. It was a hard life, but she made the best of it.

One day while she was walking home, she spied what looked like an old cooking-pot lying in the ditch.

"Well!" she said. "There's a lucky thing! I daresay the pot has a hole in it, or it wouldn't have been thrown away, but it's just the thing to stand on my window-ledge with a pot of flowers inside it." She went and looked at the pot more closely. It was full of gold pieces.

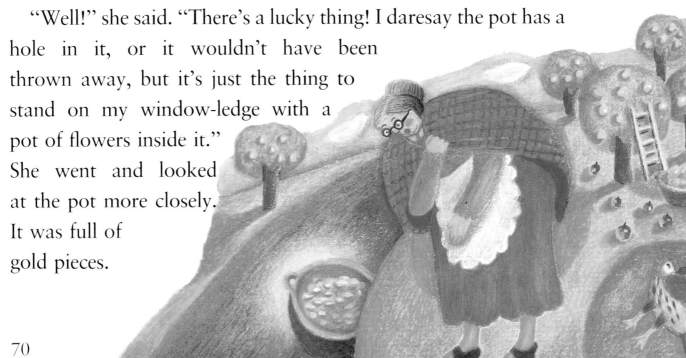

"Well!" she said. "That is a lucky thing! It's a case of finders keepers, I suppose. I shall be able to live in comfort for the rest of my days."

The pot of gold was too heavy to carry, so she tied her shawl round it and began to drag it home.

Even then it was hard work and after a while she had to stop and rest. She looked inside the pot again.

"Well!" she said. "It's not gold after all, it's silver. That's luckier still. I shouldn't have been happy with all that gold about the house. There's thieves and there's beggars and there's the neighbours getting jealous. I'll be much better off with silver."

Off she went again, with her shawl tied round the pot, dragging it along behind her.

It wasn't long before she had to stop and rest again. She went to look at the silver in the pot, and found it wasn't a pot at all, but a solid lump of iron.

"Well!" said the old woman. "I do get luckier and luckier still!

I'd never have known what to do with all that silver, for I've never had more than one silver sixpence at a time in all my life before. But a lump of iron is just what I've been needing to prop my door open, so that the sun can shine straight in."

Off she went again, with her shawl wrapped round the lump of iron, dragging it behind her. She didn't stop until she came to her own front door.

Then she bent down to untie the shawl. As soon as she had done so, the lump of iron shook itself, stood up on four long legs, gave a laugh and went galloping off into the dark.

"Well!" said the old woman. "Isn't that the luckiest thing of all! If I hadn't brought home that old iron pot – that turned out to be full of gold – that turned out to be silver – that turned out to be a lump of iron – I'd never have seen the Hedley Kow with these two eyes of mine. I must be the luckiest old woman alive."

The Hedgehog's Race

A Scottish travellers' tale

●

Duncan Williamson

If you were to travel the hills of Scotland today you would find that hedgehogs and hares live together. They're great friends. It wasn't always so...

Every morning early, old Mr Brown Hare came down from his bed in the hillside. He was bound for the farmer's field because his breakfast was turnips. He loved the young turnips coming up, the leaves. But this one morning, bright and early, as old Mr Hare came popping down the hillside, a beautiful sunny morning, the first person he met was old Mr Hedgehog. And he was crawling around the hedgerows hunting for *his* breakfast! Snails and slugs and worms which hedgehogs love to eat. Because Mr Hare was feeling very frisky this morning, he rubbed his paws together and said to himself, "Oh ho, old Mr Hedgehog! I'm going to have some fun to myself this morning!" He liked to tease old Mr Hedgehog, you know!

So when he came down to the gate leading to the farmer's field old Mr Hedgehog of course sat up with his wee pointed nose and his little short legs. And old Mr Hare said, "Good morning, Short Legs!"

Now hedgehogs are very sensitive about their short legs. And they don't like it very much when somebody talks about them, because their legs really are very short! He said, "You know, my friend Mr Hare, you are not a very nice person."

"And why," said old Mr Hare, "am I not a nice person?"

"Well," he said, "every time we meet you're always talking about my legs. I can't help it that I've got short legs, because I was born like this."

Mr Hare said, "Wouldn't you like to have long legs like me? You know I've got beautiful legs. I can run faster than anyone! Dogs can't even catch me. Wouldn't it be nice if your legs were like mine and you could run fast as the wind across the fields?"

And old Mr Hedgehog said, "Well, of course it would be nice to have long legs like you. But you see, Mr Hare, you don't need long legs to run fast, you know."

"You don't need long legs to run fast?" said old Mr Hare. "Nonsense! How in the world could you run fast with those short little legs you've got? No way could you run out of the way of a dog or a fox like me. As for me, I can run swifter than the wind!"

"Well," said old Mr Hedgehog, "you see, my friend, I'll tell you what I'll do with you. I'll make a bargain with you. I'll challenge you to a race!"

And old Mr Hare cocked up his ears and said, "Am I hearing right? You mean you're challenging me to a race!"

"Of course!" said old Mr Hedgehog. "Are you getting deaf in your old age? I said *a race*!"

He said, "You mean you want to race me?"

"Of course," said old Mr Hedgehog, "I want to race you! I want to prove to you for once and for all that even though I've got short legs, I can run faster than you."

"Never!" said old Mr Hare. "No way could you run faster than me."

"Well," said old Mr Hedgehog, "would you like to prove it?"

"Of course," said old Mr Hare, rubbing his paws in glee. "This is going to be fun! I'd love to prove it!"

"Well," said old Mr Hedgehog, "tomorrow morning at this gate I will meet you here and I will race you to the foot of the five-acre field. And I'll race you back again. And I will beat you. Will you promise me one thing?"

"Anything," said old Mr Hare, "I'll promise you!"

"That you'll never call me Short Legs again as long as you live!"

Old Mr Hare said, "Look, if you want to race me, I'll race you. And then I'll beat you like you've never been beat in all your life. And I'll go so fast you will never even see me pass you by. And after I beat you I will go on calling you Short Legs all the days of your life!"

"Well," said old Mr Hedgehog, "we'll just have to wait and see."

"Done!" said old Mr Hare. "Tomorrow morning at daybreak I'm going to teach you a lesson you will never forget!"

"Well," said old Mr Hedgehog, "we'll just have to wait and see. But remember now, Mr Hare, I'll be here."

"Oh," said old Mr Hare, "I'll be here!"

And like that off went Mr Hare for his breakfast in the farmer's turnip field.

But what do you think old Mr Hedgehog did? He toddled away back to his little nest where his old wife lived, old Mrs Hedgehog! And he said, "My dear, would you do something for me?"

Of course, old Mrs Hedgehog she loved her old husband Mr Hedgehog very much. She said, "Of course, husband, I'll do anything for you!"

He said, "You see, my dear, I've challenged Mr Hare to a race."

She said, "Husband, have you gone out of your mind? Have you gone crazy?"

"No, my dear, I've not gone crazy. But," he said, "if you will agree to help me, with your help I will teach old Mr Hare a lesson he will never forget."

She said, "What do you want me to do, husband?"

"Well," he said, "it's so simple! You know, old Mr Hare thinks he's very clever. But he's not as clever as he thinks he is. Because, like everyone else, he doesn't know you from me." (Neither do I! If you met two hedgehogs, you wouldn't know a Mr from a Mrs, would you?)

"Well," she said, "husband, what do you want me to do?"

He said, "My dear, all I want you to do is... I want you to wait till daybreak. I will wait up at the top of the gate till Mr Hare comes down from the hillside, from his bush. And I will challenge him to a race. But I'm not going to run any, and neither are you! I want you to wait at the foot of the field. And when old Mr Hare comes down to the foot of the field all you have to do is just stand up and say, "I'm here before you!" And I will wait up at the top of the gate and I won't move. Silly old Mr Hare will never know you from me!" So the plan was made.

That night, after giving her old husband Mr Hedgehog a little cuddle, off she went. And she wandered away down to the foot of the field. There she waited. It was summer time, the nights were not very long. And of course old Mr Hare was very bright in the morning. He liked to be up early, half past four when the sun came up! So old Mr Hedgehog he crawled away to the gate and there he waited. He never looked for a worm, he never looked for a snail. He waited for Mr Hare!

But soon as the sun began to rise, down came old Mr Hare so proud of himself. He was going to show old Mr Hedgehog this morning how to run! Like he'd never run before in all his life. And then he was going to go on calling him Short Legs every time they met. See? And many other things forbyes. Slow Coach and things like that! So when Mr Hare came to the gate, there sat old Mr Hedgehog.

He said, "Good morning, Short Legs, are you ready?"

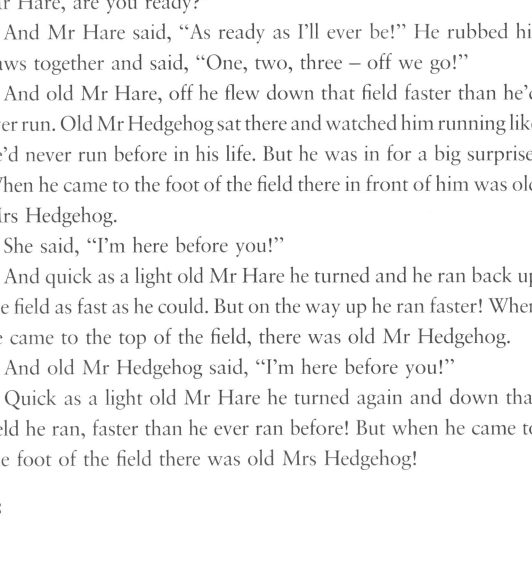

Of course, Mr Hedgehog, who was very sensitive about his short legs, said, "You promised you wouldn't call me Short Legs any more!"

He said, "Of course, I promised you – but after the race! You've not beat me yet. And you don't have one single chance in this world. I'm going to beat you, and this morning because I feel so frisky I'm going to show you what it's like to run! After I beat you I'm going to go on calling you Short Legs all your life and many other things forbyes!"

"Well," said old Mr Hedgehog, thinking to himself, "she'll be at the bottom of the field by this time." He was happy. He said, "OK, Mr Hare, are you ready?"

And Mr Hare said, "As ready as I'll ever be!" He rubbed his paws together and said, "One, two, three – off we go!"

And old Mr Hare, off he flew down that field faster than he'd ever run. Old Mr Hedgehog sat there and watched him running like he'd never run before in his life. But he was in for a big surprise. When he came to the foot of the field there in front of him was old Mrs Hedgehog.

She said, "I'm here before you!"

And quick as a light old Mr Hare he turned and he ran back up the field as fast as he could. But on the way up he ran faster! When he came to the top of the field, there was old Mr Hedgehog.

And old Mr Hedgehog said, "I'm here before you!"

Quick as a light old Mr Hare he turned again and down that field he ran, faster than he ever ran before! But when he came to the foot of the field there was old Mrs Hedgehog!

She said, "I'm here before you!" And of course poor old Mr Hare, not knowing Mrs Hedgehog from Mr Hedgehog, he turned again! Up that field he flew as fast as he could run.

But then old Mr Hedgehog said, "I'm still here before you!"

So up and down and up and down ran old Mr Hare. Till at last he was completely exhausted. He could not run another step. He came up to the top of the field and he was lying there, his tongue hanging out. And he was panting.

He said, "Tell me, Mr Hedgehog, tell me, please! How in the world did you ever do it? You ran so fast I never even saw you pass me by!"

"Of course," said old Mr Hedgehog, "I told you! You wouldn't believe me that you don't need long legs to run fast, you know!"

"Well," said old Mr Hare, "you really beat me there and I'm still not sure how you did it, but I promise you, my friend, I will never call you Short Legs again as long as I live!"

And that's why today, if you're up in the gorse hills, in the woods, you will find hedgehogs and hares asleep in the same bush – because they are very good friends! And as for old Mr Hare, he never called Mr Hedgehog Short Legs again. But of course you and I know that he beat him by a trick, didn't he? But we ain't going to tell Mr Hare, are we?

Rainbow Bird

An Aboriginal story

•

Eric Maddern

A long time ago, so the old people say, there was a big, big, big, Crocodile. He had tough, scaly skin and razorsharp teeth, and he was really, really mean. And this Crocodile Man had one thing no one else had. Just like a dragon he had fire! But he used to sit by his billabong all day long and keep the fire to himself. "I'm boss for fire," he would growl at the other animals. "I'm boss for fire."

Now in a nearby tree lived the Plain Bird Woman. Plain Bird Woman had no light. At night she slept beside no camp fire and she had to eat her food – her fish, her lizards and her mussels – all raw! Ugh! She didn't like the taste very much, but every time she asked Crocodile Man if she could have some fire she was knocked away.

"But what about people?" she said. "Are they to eat their food raw?"

"They can eat it raw," said the gruff old Crocodile Man. "I will not give you my firesticks. I'm boss for fire."

Plain Bird Woman flew up to the nearby tree and watched Crocodile Man. She wished and wished she could have fire to cook her food and keep herself warm. Then she thought, Maybe I could just fly down and sn...sn...sn...snatch the fire from the cr...cr...cr...crocodile." She was very frightened but she got herself ready and then flew down.

"Oh no, no, no, NO!" roared the Crocodile Man. "You're just a little bird. Me, I'm a big crocodile. You must eat your food raw!"

"You're so mean," sighed Plain Bird Woman. "If I had fire I'd give it to you." And she flew back into the tree.

Time passed. Plain Bird Woman watched and waited, waited and watched. Then one day she saw Crocodile Man open his jaws and give a big yawn. "Now's my chance," she thought, and she flashed down from the tree, snatched the firesticks and flew up into the air. And there was nothing the Crocodile Man could do about it.

"Now I have light, now I can cook fish and now I shall give fire to people," said Plain Bird Woman happily. And she flew around the country putting fire at the heart of every tree, one by one. Then she flew back to Crocodile Man and said, "Now you must stay down there in the wet places. I'll fly high in the dry places. I'll be a bird. I'll stay on top. If you come up here you might die!"

And then Plain Bird Woman put the firesticks into her tail, and that's where they are today. She looked so beautiful, with the colours of fire in her feathers, that everyone called her 'Rainbow Bird'. Even today, in Australia, she's known as the 'Rainbow Lorikeet'.

And now if you want to make fire, what do you need?

Matches! And what are the matches made from? Wood! And where does the wood come from? Trees! And what's in the heart of the tree? Fire! And who put the fire into the heart of the tree? The Rainbow Bird!

Papa Bwa Greedy Guest

A story from Dominica

•

Jane Grell

A woodcutter came home one night with a very strange old man. His hair was thick and tangled like a wild overgrown garden. His bushy grey beard was so long it almost touched the ground.

"This is Papa Bwa," said the woodcutter, introducing the old man to his wife, Nana. "His job is to protect the forest and everything in it. At least that's what he told me."

"Then why have you brought him here?" asked his wife, not very pleased to see the old man.

"He is very, very hungry," replied the wood-cutter, "so I've invited him to supper."

Nana his wife could not easily turn away a hungry old man from her house, but she was far from happy.

"Hmm!" she said at last. "He'll have to wash and change into something cleaner. There's a tub of water out there," she said to the old man and pointed to the yard. "And you better put these on." She handed him an old pair of clean overalls.

After he had washed and changed she was still not satisfied. She looked the old man up and down and sucked her teeth in disgust.

"Chut, man, this beard has got to go. There must be a million bugs and fleas hiding in there. I'm not having them crawling all over my house, you hear."

So Papa Bwa had to agree to cut off his beard before he could sit down to supper of fried dumplings and hot chocolate, smelling so delicious from the kitchen.

After supper Papa Bwa curled up on a small sofa and went to sleep.

At breakfast the next morning a very odd thing happened. When Nana gave Papa Bwa a mug of tea, he drank the tea and ate the mug.

At lunchtime Nana gave him fried plantains and flying fish on a dish. Papa Bwa ate the food and devoured the dish.

At suppertime Nana gave him calaloo and crab in a calabash. Papa Bwa gobbled up the calaloo and crab and polished off the calabash.

The next morning Nana gave him tea in a zinc jug. He gulped down the tea and crunched away the jug.

At lunch that day Nana gave him rice and peas and avocado on a plate. He wolfed down the rice and peas and avocado and munched away the plate.

That night Nana gave him supper of pigeon peas with curried salt fish in a wooden washing-up bowl. Papa Bwa enjoyed the pigeon peas and curried salt fish then guzzled up the washing-up bowl.

Papa Bwa stayed several days with the woodcutter and his wife and during that time he ate his way through several mugs, jugs, a calabash, a washing-up bowl, a bucket and even a pig's trough.

Nana was very upset. One night she said to her husband, "Tomorrow, you must take this . . . creature back to the woods where you found him and leave him there."

"But supposing he follows me back?" said the woodcutter.

"You found him," yelled his wife impatiently, "you get rid of him. If you don't, we won't have a single cup or plate left in this house. The way he's going, who knows? He'll eat all the furniture, then the house and he will surely eat us as well."

For once the woodcutter listened to his wife. He did not want his chairs, table and bed to be eaten. He did not much want his wife to be eaten and he certainly did not like the idea of being eaten himself.

So early in the morning he told Papa Bwa that it was time to return to his home in the forest as he made his wife very unhappy.

Papa Bwa went quietly with the woodcutter until they reached the spot in the woods where they had met, then he demanded to have his beard back. "I will not go without my beard!" he shrieked.

"But that's impossible," replied the woodcutter. "Your beard has been cut off and is lying on a rubbish heap under a mango tree."

But the old man only stamped his feet shouting, "I don't care!" Then he started jumping up and down, up and down in front of the woodcutter, chanting:

"CRICK! CRACK!
BREAK MY BACK
I WANT MY BEARD
AND THAT IS THAT."

Suddenly, from somewhere in the forest, appeared three wise old women of the woods. They wanted to know what the argument was about, so the woodcutter told them everything and Papa Bwa finished up with:

"CRICK! CRACK!
BREAK MY BACK
I WANT MY BEARD
AND THAT IS THAT."

The three wise women of the woods shrieked with laughter and delight and they too started to jump around singing:

"CRICK! CRACK!
BREAK HIS BACK
HE WANTS HIS BEARD
AND THAT IS THAT."

Well, they chanted and clapped and danced round and round the poor woodcutter until he was quite dizzy.

Just then a bird swept down from the tree tops. It was Siflet Montagne, the beautiful whistling bird of the mountains. She was curious to know what all the singing and dancing was about. So the woodcutter told the whole story all over again, finished off by Papa Bwa with:

> "CRICK! CRACK!
> BREAK MY BACK
> I WANT MY BEARD
> AND THAT IS THAT."

helped along by the three wise women of the woods with:

> "CRICK! CRACK!
> BREAK HIS BACK
> HE WANTS HIS BEARD
> AND THAT IS THAT."

The mountain whistler felt sorry for the woodcutter and wanted to help him. So she whistled in her most melodious voice while the dancers whirled and swirled, danced and pranced, jigged and jogged to the fabulous tune of this enchanting bird.

Then the mountain whistler hovered close to the woodcutter and whispered, "I will whistle for a little while more. When they are not looking, you must seize your chance and run for it, man."

Then the bird sang more sweetly and the dancers danced more quickly as they followed her down the path.

"CRICK! CRACK!

BREAK MY BACK

I WANT MY BEARD

AND THAT IS THAT."

And as they skipped and bopped, hipped and hopped, wheeled and turned, led away by the whistling bird, the woodcutter saw his chance and VOOP! he slipped away towards his own cottage. But he hadn't gone very far when Papa Bwa and the three wise women of the woods realized what was happening. VOOP! they left the mountain whistler and began to chase the woodcutter, who ran and ran and ran, and never stopped until he was safely home. There, his wife Nana was standing in the open doorway. He rushed in, pulling her along with him and bolted the door just in the nick of time, the nick of time, leaving his shirt in the grasping hands of the fastest wise woman of the woods.

From that day on, the woodcutter and his wife have been *very* careful about inviting strangers home to supper.

Cherry Tree Hill

An Australian settlers' yarn

•

Helen East

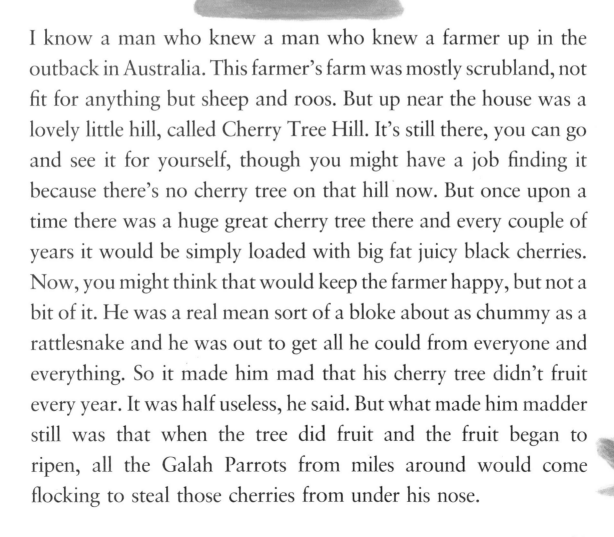

I know a man who knew a man who knew a farmer up in the outback in Australia. This farmer's farm was mostly scrubland, not fit for anything but sheep and roos. But up near the house was a lovely little hill, called Cherry Tree Hill. It's still there, you can go and see it for yourself, though you might have a job finding it because there's no cherry tree on that hill now. But once upon a time there was a huge great cherry tree there and every couple of years it would be simply loaded with big fat juicy black cherries. Now, you might think that would keep the farmer happy, but not a bit of it. He was a real mean sort of a bloke about as chummy as a rattlesnake and he was out to get all he could from everyone and everything. So it made him mad that his cherry tree didn't fruit every year. It was half useless, he said. But what made him madder still was that when the tree did fruit and the fruit began to ripen, all the Galah Parrots from miles around would come flocking to steal those cherries from under his nose.

He'd try everything to scare them off – scarecrows, jangling cans, nets, wires, the lot. He even had his little son out morning, noon and night, trying to knock those birds down with his catapult. "Dollar a dozen dead'uns," the farmer promised but his son never got even a penny, for those Galahs were harder to catch than the Devil himself. They would wait till the boy was almost on them and then they would sidestep or swing or simply flap to safety, shrieking with raucous laughter. And the farmer got madder than mad just watching them.

So now one year he said to his wife, "This time those Galahs are gonna get it 'cause this time I'll dang well give it to them meself!"

And he took his gun and parked himself right under that tree and he waited. Well, he waited one day, two days, three days, and he waited one night, two nights, three nights, but all he got was a stiff neck, a sore head and a worse temper. Those Galahs had spotted him from miles away and they just kept a safe distance and bided their time.

"Drat those darn Galahs!" the farmer snarled as he

stamped off home for a drink and a think. And then, out of the blue, it just came to him. A real dingo of a plan! A way to get the lot at once – and it couldn't fail! For the first time in years, the farmer grinned. He went back to the house, got out his truck and drove the eighty miles in to the nearest town. When he got back he had a great big barrel up on the seat beside him and he was still grinning. But he wouldn't let on to anyone what was up. He just bided his time, watched the Galahs flocking round the tree, and grinned till you'd think his face would split.

Well, that night, when everyone else was asleep, the farmer got the barrel out and rolled it up the hill. As soon as he got near the tree, the Galahs, asleep on the branches, woke up and flew quickly out of reach. But the farmer didn't care. He just opened up his barrel, picked up a paintbrush, dipped it in and began to paint that cherry tree, very carefully, all over, from the top down to the bottom. And when every branch and every twig and every leaf was covered the farmer threw away the empty barrel, washed his hands and went home to bed.

As soon as the farmer was safely gone, the roosting Galahs returned to the tree. When dawn came their friends and relatives came to join them for breakfast and as the morning wore on latecomers from more distant parts arrived in cheery cackling crowds. Yet still the farmer slept on. By the time he finally woke up, around noon, the tree was so laden with birds you could hardly see the cherries and the farmer's family had given up hoping for any fruit at all that year. But the farmer just grinned, and loaded his gun.

"I said I'd get them Galahs and I'm gonna get them good!" he said. And out he went, with his son at his heels.

Well, the Galahs saw them coming, of course, but they weren't worried. They had plenty of time to finish feasting before the farmer got too close. It wasn't until he was halfway up the hill that one old bird roused herself and gave the call to the others. "Better move along, boys," and she lazily flapped her wings.

But oh! What was this? Her wings moved but her feet stayed right where they were, held fast to the branch. For do you know what the farmer had painted that cherry tree with so carefully? Glue! The stickiest, stretchiest, strongest glue you ever could imagine. And of course those Galahs had settled right on it and now they were stuck tight.

And the farmer thought it was the funniest sight he had ever seen. The harder those birds flapped, and the louder they squawked, the more he liked it. He was laughing so much he could hardly point his gun. Bang! His first shot went right up into the air. Didn't so much as graze one wing but it put the Galahs into even more of a panic. And they flapped so wildly the wind whistled through the leaves, and the cherries were blown this way and that, and the branches were weaving and crashing and thrashing. And they flapped so frantically the tree itself began to sway and to swirl and to turn and to lift until, with a tremendous tearing roar, the roots were ripped right out of the ground and the tree rose into the air. Up! Up! Up! Carried by the beating wings of a thousand grateful Galahs.

As for the farmer and his son, they were so astonished they were rooted to the spot, gawping goggle-eyed, till the birds and their burden were no more than a speck in the sky. And all that was left of the cherry tree was the name of the hill and a darn great gaping hole.

But as for the Galahs, some people say that they are flying to this day. So next time you think you see a plane – rub your eyes and look again.